CW00517921

BRIAN JOHNSTON

Not Fake News!

HAYES
PRESS Christian Publisher

Contents

1

Not Fake News

We've all heard the term 'fake news' - Donald Trump made sure we did. If something's fake, we can be sure it's false. There's a true story about an elderly gentleman who was preaching one Sunday evening in the south of England. He became quite animated during his presentation of God's Good News as found in the Bible; so animated, in fact, that at one point his full set of false teeth flew out of his mouth and clattered onto the floor. With no more ado, he calmly descended from the pulpit and collected his teeth from the floor in front of his audience. By the time he'd returned to the pulpit and was facing his audience once more, the teeth were already back in his mouth, and he continued quite unfazed by announcing to his spell-bound listeners: 'There's nothing false about the Gospel!' I would have to say that such presence of mind more than compensated for the brief absence of teeth!

But we were talking about how fake news is trending. Some of it is as dangerous as it's bizarre, shown most recently by anti-vaxxers. Lies, of course, of whatever type, are far from new.

Take the story told of the rough-looking group of boys who encountered a church minister. He saw they had a dog on the end of a piece of string. "Hey, what are you boys doing with that dog?" for it looked to him as if it was a stray dog. "We found this dog, mister, and we've all agreed that the one who tells the biggest lie gets to keep it." The church minister reacted with shock horror: "Boys, that's not a good thing to do! You shouldn't be encouraging each other to tell lies. Lies are bad, and do a lot of harm. Listen to me when I tell you this: by the time I was your age I'd never told a single lie." At this the leading boy was downcast. He nodded to the boy holding the dog, "Wow! That's a corker, guys. We're never gonna beat that one - just give him the dog!"

We're talking about commandment #9 of the famous biblical Ten: *"You shall not bear false witness."* At the time of writing, in the UK there's the possibility of a court case involving someone in the royal family about a very unsavoury matter, and for sure one side or the other is telling lies. Then there's also what's happening in the British Parliament at Westminster. It's like a 'soap opera' all about alleged lies and the government breaking its own rules. It used to be portrayed like this in a British television comedy show called 'Yes, Minister', but now it seems to be real life in No.10 Downing Street – with all the allegations of the so-called Partygate. And, it's not funny - it's tragic for so many people who have lost loved ones (when keeping the rules).

But I want to mention what I consider to be the biggest lie in the world. It's found in different cultures and religions, and this is what it says: "If you do the best you can in life, when you stand before God, he'll weigh up all the good things you've ever done and all the bad things you've ever done, and if the good outweighs the bad, then he'll let you into heaven." That's not the Good News of the Bible. That's fake news. The Bible says (in Galatians 2:16): *"a person is not justified by works of the Law but through faith in Christ Jesus, even we have believed in Christ Jesus, so that we may be justified by faith in Christ and not by works of the Law; since by works of the Law no flesh will be justified."*

What that's telling us is that in all of history there's not been one single person born with a human father who has been acceptable to God as a result of their good deeds. This false news of the good outweighing the bad, can easily be shown to be a foolish idea. Take the motorcycle thief who appears before the magistrate and demands justice. "Excuse me?" the judge says. "Justice? What on earth do you mean? Did you or did you not steal your neighbour's motorbike on the 15th of May last year?" "Yes, your honour, I did, but will you not bear in mind that there were another 364 days last year when I did NOT steal his motorbike, so I want justice!" Crazy, isn't it?

Remember the rich man in the Bible (Matthew 19) who claimed to Jesus that he'd kept all the commandments (that was a lie, but a sincere one)? Jesus then told him to go and sell all he had and give it away to the poor. But, even if he'd donated everything to the poor, it still wouldn't have saved him. Jesus was simply testing – demonstrating the impossibility of any of us earning our place in eternity with God, no matter what apparently awesome thing we do. But when talking with my neighbour Mohammed recently, it dawned on me there's another lie that's equal to the one mentioned. He asked me about Jesus and what I thought of Islam, and I directed him to his phone where he had a copy of the Qur'an. I asked if he agreed with Surah 4 verse 157 that states the lie that Jesus did not die. The Apostle Paul wrote in the Bible that if we could make ourselves acceptable to God by our own religious good works then it would mean there was no need for Christ to have died. To think we can make ourselves acceptable to God by ourselves is the same as the lie that denies Jesus died for us.

In conversation in some countries where we're working, it's popular to ask: "If you were standing at heaven's door and were asked 'Why should you be allowed to enter?' what would you say?' Those who have believed the lie will say "Because of my good life." Those who have denied Christ's death and its relevance, will say "Because of my own good works." But the successful candidate follows the example of the dying thief who repented of all his sins and called on Jesus. His answer could only be: "I'm here because the man on the centre cross said I could come!" Shall we remind ourselves of what happened the day Jesus died?

> *"And when they came to the place called The Skull, there they crucified Him and the criminals, one on the right and the other on the left. [But Jesus was saying, 'Father, forgive them; for they do not know what they are doing.'] And they cast lots, dividing His garments among themselves. And the people stood by, watching. And even the rulers were sneering at Him, saying, 'He saved others; let Him save Himself if this is the Christ of God, His Chosen One.' The soldiers also ridiculed Him, coming up to Him, offering Him sour wine, and saying, 'If You are the King of the Jews, save Yourself!' Now there*

was also an inscription above Him, 'THIS IS THE KING OF THE JEWS.'

One of the criminals who were hanged there was hurling abuse at Him, saying, 'Are You not the Christ? Save Yourself and us!' But the other responded, and rebuking him, said, 'Do you not even fear God, since you are under the same sentence of condemnation? And we indeed are suffering justly, for we are receiving what we deserve for our crimes; but this man has done nothing wrong.' And he was saying, 'Jesus, remember me when You come into Your kingdom!' And He said to him, 'Truly I say to you, today you will be with Me in Paradise' (Luke 23:33-43).

So, now, if you were asked: "If you were standing at heaven's door and were asked 'Why should you be allowed to enter?' what would you say? Will you follow the example of that dying thief who repented of all his sins and called in faith on Jesus? Will you answer: "I'm only here because the man on the centre cross said I could come!"?

2

Does It Matter Who We Worship?

The news at the time of writing is dominated by the war caused by Russia's invasion of neighbouring Ukraine. Daily, our news media's headlines are full of reports of the inhumane horrors of the indiscriminate killings of children and hospital patients. I'm reminded of the poet, Steve Turner, who wrote:

> *If chance be the Father of all flesh,*
> *disaster is his rainbow in the sky,*
> *and when you hear*
> *State of Emergency!*
> *Sniper Kills Ten!*
> *Troops on Rampage!*
> *Whites go Looting!*
> *Bomb Blasts School!*
> *It is but the sound of man worshiping his maker.*

If chance is the father of us all … poet Turner reasons. A scientist who believed in the chance origin of life, the universe and in fact of all things once said: "We are here because one odd group of fishes had a peculiar fin anatomy that could transform into legs for terrestrial creatures; because comets struck the earth and wiped out dinosaurs, thereby giving mammals a chance not otherwise available (so thank your lucky stars in a literal sense); because the earth never froze entirely during an ice age; because a small and tenuous species, arising in Africa a quarter of a million years ago, has managed, so far, to survive by hook and by crook. We may yearn for a "higher" answer – but none exists. This explanation, though superficially troubling, if not terrifying, is ultimately liberating and exhilarating" (Stephen Jay Gould). Let's read Turner's poetry again ...

> *If chance be the Father of all flesh,*
> *Disaster is his rainbow in the sky,*
> *And when you hear*
> *State of Emergency!*
> *Sniper Kills Ten!*
> *Troops on Rampage!*
> *Whites go Looting!*
> *Bomb Blasts School!*
> *It is but the sound of man worshiping his maker.*

That's the direct result of people believing that we are here by chance with no higher power to whom we will one day be held accountable. The sound of war and injustice in the world today – is this the sound of humanity worshiping its maker? This is the world that practical atheism arrives at. But let me ask you: "Does that really sound exhilarating to you?" Or does it better expose the condition of the human heart? A heart that has alienated itself from God: the result of those who say in their heart that there is no God. That's what they say in their heart but the heart is deceitful above all things (Jeremiah 17:9).

There's a story of a little boy in India who had lots of rather nice marbles. But he was jealous – of all things - of his sister's bag of sweets. So he said to her, "Let's do a deal. If you give me all your sweets, I'll give you all my marbles." She thought about it and agreed to the swap. So he took her sweets, all of them of course, and went back to his room to fetch his marbles by way of exchange. But, the more he looked at them, the more reluctant he was to give them all up. So he took the best ones and put them under his pillow, and only took the remainder to give to his sister. Well, that night she slept soundly while he tossed and turned restlessly, unable to sleep – all the while thinking, "I wonder if she gave me **_all_** the sweets."

Let me ask you this: "Have you seen your own heart?" When we doubt others – and maybe even God – think about it. Could it be we're really acknowledging our own deceitfulness? The boy wouldn't have doubted his sister if he'd not been all too aware of his own deceit in the matter. And our suspicions are usually well-founded; because all hearts are like our own heart – which is basically deceitful. Is that a bit too harsh? Well, no, for Jeremiah the Bible prophet says: *"The heart is more deceitful than all else ..."* (17:9). And so I ask – I ask every one of us again: "Have you seen your own heart?"

At the time of writing this, I've just returned from a country in the Far East. After one's night's sharing of God's Good News up in a hillside village on a starlit tropical night, one woman at the back of the group started to sob. It began towards the close of the preaching that night. Later, she was asked why she had been crying. This was her answer: she said "I was overwhelmed by a sense of my sin." She had seen her own heart. Before God will change anyone's life, they've first to realize what the heart of their problem is – it's the problem of their heart! Not that you're able to change it for yourself. I read once that the former world boxing champion Muhammad Ali refused to fasten his seat-belt during turbulence on an airplane. He said to the air stewardess – with the quick wit he was famous for - "Superman need no seat-belt." But the stewardess was equal to him that day and back she came at once with: "Superman also need no airplane – so you will please fasten your belt"! We are no super-men and -women in God's sight, because he sees our heart. And what's more, we can do nothing about the state of it.

Maybe you've heard of someone who's been styled as the world's least successful kite-flier? Apparently, he was a Californian whose kite hit a high voltage power cable. It caught fire and came crashing down to earth where it started a fire that damaged 385 homes, 740 acres of scrub-land, and caused 3,000 people to be evacuated. The bill? Twenty million dollars. Now what does your average guy do? Reach for his chequebook? No, I don't think so. Nor is it any more realistic to offer to come every weekend with your paintbrush and tools and try to make it right all by yourself. Meeting that kind of debt is overwhelmingly beyond us. Our indebtedness to God because of the deceitfulness of our heart is something we can do nothing about. Our heart, the Bible says, is desperately sick' (Jeremiah 17:9). Its condition is way beyond critical - it's desperate, and no religious therapy of any kind can cure it.

The story's told of two brothers who were notorious gang

members. When one died the other went to a pastor and asked if he would take his brother's funeral. He offered the pastor a great deal of money for doing so – upon one condition: that at some point in his sermon the pastor would speak of this rogue as a saint. The pastor said he felt he could just about manage that. When the day came the pastor waxed eloquent about the vile character of the deceased. This man, he said, was rotten to the core of his being, capable of – and indeed guilty of – the most horrific crimes. But compared to his brother he was a saint!

Have you seen your own heart? Who do you compare yourself with? Compared to whom are you a saint? When we compare ourselves with a Hitler or a Stalin, we feel pretty comfortable with the idea of ultimate justice, don't we? But when we compare ourselves to the standards we glimpse in the Bible, we sense how much we stand in need of God's mercy. What God asks us to do is to turn from our self-centred, self-choosing, self-serving ways and come to Christ, just as we are, because he'll change us – but come believing that the only remedy to the problem of your heart lies in the provision of God's own heart through the cross.

Those who come to Christ find completeness in the one who declared himself to be the way, the truth and the life. When a person acknowledges God and Christ as his Saviour, what a difference it makes and what a difference it would make to our society if there was a genuine revival of belief in God over against the hopeless belief in chance. For Christian worship has been aptly described as:

The quickening of our conscience by his holiness
The nourishing of our minds by his truth

The enlarging of our hearts by his love
The purifying of our imagination by his beauty
The submission of our wills to his purpose.

How different today's world would be if all or most were truly worshiping the real creator God.

3

Lost & Found

It's common knowledge that Jesus told stories known as parables. Strictly speaking, these parables were not allegories, which is where everything has an alternative meaning (making an allegory a sort of extended metaphor). Parables, or at least many of them, were really more like a kind of pointed joke at someone's expense – a story that's getting at someone by means of leading up to a very loaded punch-line. Very often, Jesus' critics, the Pharisees and other religious groups, were the target of his parables. I would now like to share some thoughts on one of Jesus' famous stories. This is what Jesus said, as recorded in Luke's Gospel, chapter 15:

> "Or what woman, if she has ten silver coins and loses one coin, does not light a lamp and sweep the house and search carefully until she finds it? When she has found it, she calls together her friends and neighbours, saying, 'Rejoice with me, for I have found the coin which I had lost!' In the same way, I tell you, there is joy in the presence of the angels of God over one sinner who

repents."

The telling of this story is part of Jesus' response to the criticism made against him by religious leaders when they said Jesus was a friend of tax-gatherers and blatant sinners. You'll gather they didn't like the tax-collectors in those days. There was an extra reason for that, one that went beyond any dislike in handing over hard-earned money to the government. These tax-gatherers were considered traitors to their own nation because they were in the employment of the occupying Roman power. Not only that, but they charged the people more than they should and put the extra into their own pockets. It's hardly surprising then that they weren't liked and that their behaviour was viewed as despicable. But what they did do was that they listened to Jesus, and he would at times have meals with them. This was too much for the Pharisees and other religious groups to tolerate and so they criticised Jesus for this – which as we say led Jesus to tell this story against them.

The nine coins which the woman didn't lose serve as a reference to the Pharisees. The one lost coin refers to the tax-collectors and sinners – those whom the religious leaders back then couldn't be bothered with; quite frankly, they thought they were a waste of space. So Jesus is now about to use this story as a shock tactic to face those religious people up with the fact that theirs was not God's valuation of the tax-collectors and other 'big' sinners. Before we go further, as we consider this story I want to suggest it gives us all 4 things to think about. Here are four messages from it:

1. You are valuable...

2. but could it be that you are lost?
3. However, if God is looking for you …
4. then might this be your opportunity to repent?

Let's get started. Remember how in the story told by Jesus the woman continued to sweep the house and search carefully until she found the coin which was a thing of great value. The coin in question which she'd lost was a 'drachma', a Greek silver coin which is only referred to here in all of the New Testament. This coin equalled about a full day's wages. Now remember how we said that this one lost coin referred to the sinners whom the religious leaders despised? The point would have been clear to Jesus' listeners: the sinners with whom Jesus was associating were being portrayed as being extremely valuable to God (Cf. similar wording in vv.6,9).

But we said we're also trying to connect with this story for any contemporary significance. Let's explore the overall message that you, too, really matter, and so need to be found. You're valuable to God! The story is told of a man who loved old books. He met an acquaintance who told him he'd just thrown away a Bible that'd been stored in the attic of his ancestral home for generations. "I couldn't read it," the friend explained. "Somebody named Guten-something had printed it." "Not Gutenberg!" the book-lover exclaimed in horror. "That Bible was one of the first books ever printed. Why, a copy just sold for over two million dollars!" His friend was unimpressed. "Mine wouldn't have fetched a single dollar. Some fellow named Martin Luther had scribbled all over it in German" (*Our Daily Bread*, June 7, 1994).

Of course, Martin Luther was the famous German Reformer, and any copy of an early printed Bible with his handwritten notes would be a highly sought-after collector's item! But, so the story goes, the person who found this book was ignorant of these matters, and therefore to him it was simply an old book with little or no value. Similarly, you might not think you matter to God, but you are valuable in God's sight. You might dismiss the idea that God could be interested in you. But if so, then you need to understand this story to discover you really are valuable to God. But not only valuable, but lost!

The famous author Orwell describes a wasp which he said "was sucking jam on my plate and I cut him in half. The wasp paid no attention, merely went on with his meal, while a tiny stream of jam trickled out of his severed oesophagus. Only when he tried to fly away did he grasp the dreadful thing that had happened to him." That wasp and people without Christ have much in common. Severed from their souls, still greedy and unaware, people continue to consume life's sweetness. Only when it's time to fly away might they grasp their dreadful condition.

But some even with their last breath are oblivious to their state: The circus magnate P. T. Barnum on his deathbed asked: "How are the circus receipts today?" But so you may not be oblivious like that to the true state of affairs, we ask: "How do you know if you're lost?" We're going to take our answers to that question from Ephesians 4. It's there that Paul describes 'lost people' as being of a futile mind – in other words, their lives are devoid of God's purpose. Paul next writes about their darkened understanding – meaning they're without God's revelation to guide or enlighten them. Then Paul goes on to say that they've got hardened hearts – in other words, they're insensitive to God and his ways. Finally, Paul mentions impure greed and deceitful lusts – which means lost people are living for self-gratification in some form. Please consider if these things could possibly describe you.

Well, it's time to get back to the parable. In the parable, the woman had to light a lamp in the darkened room of her house and painstakingly she began to search for the coin. Her trustworthiness is on the line. This makes a difference between the story of the lost coin and the other two stories of lost things which Jesus told in Luke chapter 15: namely about the lost sheep and the lost son. The shepherd didn't lose the sheep, nor did the father lose the son, but this woman lost the coin. She'd been entrusted with the money and was responsible for it. She needs to find it, and she knows the coin must be in the house. If she looks hard enough, she realizes, the coin can surely be found.

I wonder if you're also willing to take responsibility for the way you are? Perhaps, you're lost - but there's hope. If God's looking for you, you'll be found. There's that certainty for all those who belong to him. Perhaps, this is your opportunity to repent? Let me try to illustrate for you what it means to repent, because we need to understand what God is calling upon us to do. Ernest Miller Hemingway (July 21, 1899 - July 2, 1961) was an American author who died as a result of a self-inflicted shotgun blast to the head. That shotgun had previously been his young son's proud boast, a possession he'd taken pleasure in, something he could brag about to his friends. But after that fateful day when his father used it to end his own life, the boy's attitude towards the gun changed completely. His mother told him to take it and throw it into the lake. He did so. The thing he'd previously taken such delight in, the trophy that had adorned their house, and in the young's boy's thinking at least had once deserved pride of place was now a hated object. What had brought about such a reversal of opinion, such a total change of attitude? It was because when he looked at the gun, what he now saw was the very weapon that had taken his dear father's life. From being something he'd been proud of, that gun was now something he hated.

So, when the Bible calls on us to repent of our sin, it means we're no longer to take pleasure in sin as we once did, but now instead to hate it since it was our sin which led Christ to die on the cross for us. To truly repent first means that we recognize that we've done wrong. But for some it's possible to recognize wrong-doing but not be sorry for the sin – only for the fact they've been caught. Repentance, therefore, also includes remorse, which is to be sorry for what we've done. Again, some may get that far, but stop short at begging for forgiveness. It's as if they can admit their shameful guilt to themselves but not to others. So, repentance involves a recognition of having done wrong, having remorse for it, as well as requesting forgiveness. Some may even go that far, but they're thinking 'given half a chance I'd do it again'! That kind of attitude also is one that stops short of repentance. True repentance definitely includes a preparedness to renounce what we've done. That is, to take the view: "I've learnt my lesson, and I aim never to do the same thing again." But there also needs to be a readiness to restore or hand back anything by which our actions have defrauded others of what's rightfully theirs.

As you read this now, I hope you'll remember the value of the lost coin, and realise that you really do matter to God. Then, remember the woman searching for that coin and realize that God's looking for – and missing – you. Remember, finally, the joy of the woman when she found her lost coin, and the joy there will be in heaven when you turn to God. You now have an opportunity to take responsibility and repent. Will you take it?

4

Dead Man Walking

A man working in the produce department was asked by a lady if she could buy half a head of lettuce. He replied, "Half a head? Are you serious? God grows these in whole heads and that's how we sell them!" "You mean," she persisted, "that after all the years I've shopped here, you won't sell me half-a-head of lettuce?" "Look," he said, "if you like I'll ask the manager." She indicated that would be appreciated, so the young man marched to the front of the store to where his manager was located. "You won't believe this, but there's a lame-brained idiot of a lady back there who wants to know if she can buy half-a-head of lettuce." He noticed the manager's face turn red and he started gesturing. So, he turned around to see the lady standing behind him, obviously having followed him to the front of the store. He immediately recovered himself and said: "And this nice lady was wondering if she could buy the other half," he concluded. Later in the day the manager cornered the young man and said, "That was the finest example of thinking on your feet I've ever seen! Where did you learn that?" "I grew up in Grand Rapids, and if you know anything about Grand Rapids you know that it's known for its great hockey teams and its ugly women." The manager's face flushed, and he interrupted, "My wife is from Grand Rapids!" "And which hockey team did she play for?" was the young man's reply.

In the early part of 2014 there may have been times when the French President wished he'd had such diplomatic nimbleness. He could have used it when he was attempting damage limitation in the romantic muddle he'd got himself into. Instead, he appeared to fumble. Followers of France's political love story may have been intrigued by some expressions he used in the media. What, for example, did they make of a presidential statement that the woman he'd previously been associated with had succumbed to 'the blues'? It seemed callous to underplay the extent of her distress. You wouldn't normally go to hospital with a case of 'the blues,' but this jilted companion had been hospitalised. But enough of that. One of the Bible's great characters, Abraham, made a bigger blunder by far in relation to the statements he made about the most important woman in his life, his wife, Sarah. Here we have it recorded for us in Genesis 20:

> *"Now Abraham journeyed from there toward the land of the Negev, and settled between Kadesh and Shur; then he sojourned in Gerar. Abraham said of Sarah his wife, 'She is my sister.' So Abimelech king of Gerar sent and took Sarah. But God came to Abimelech in a dream of the night, and said to him, 'Behold, you are a dead man because of the woman whom you have taken, for she is married.' Now Abimelech had not come near her; and he said, 'Lord, will You slay a nation, even though blameless? Did he*

not himself say to me, "She is my sister"? And she herself said, "He is my brother." In the integrity of my heart and the innocence of my hands I have done this."

Then God said to him in the dream, 'Yes, I know that in the integrity of your heart you have done this, and I also kept you from sinning against Me; therefore I did not let you touch her. Now therefore, restore the man's wife, for he is a prophet, and he will pray for you and you will live. But if you do not restore her, know that you shall surely die, you and all who are yours.' So Abimelech arose early in the morning and called all his servants and told all these things in their hearing; and the men were greatly frightened. Then Abimelech called Abraham and said to him, 'What have you done to us? And how have I sinned against you, that you have brought on me and on my kingdom a great sin? You have done to me things that ought not to be done.'

And Abimelech said to Abraham, 'What have you encountered, that you have done this thing?' Abraham said, 'Because I thought, surely there is no fear of God in this place, and they will kill me because of my wife. Besides, she actually is my sister, the daughter of my father, but not the daughter of my mother, and she became my wife; and it came about, when God caused me to wander from my father's house, that I said to her, "This is the kindness which you will show to me: everywhere we go, say of me, 'He is my brother.'"' Abimelech then took sheep and oxen and male and female servants, and gave them to Abraham, and restored his wife Sarah to him. Abimelech said, 'Behold, my land is before you; settle wherever you please.'

To Sarah he said, 'Behold, I have given your brother a thousand pieces of silver; behold, it is your vindication before all who are with you, and before all men you are cleared. Abraham prayed to God, and God healed Abimelech and his wife and his maids, so that they bore children.' For the LORD had closed fast all the wombs of the household of Abimelech because of Sarah, Abraham's wife" (Genesis 20:1-18).

This was certainly not Abraham's finest hour, not his most glorious moment. His lack of courage here borders on cowardice. The faith for which this man is justly renowned is nowhere in evidence here and any semblance of chivalry has disappeared right out the window. It is just as well for Abraham that God was taking care of him. Indeed, Abimelech comes out of this episode with much more credit than Abraham. But what a shock it must have been for him to have God come to him in a dream and tell him "you are a dead man" – and that because he'd innocently taken Abraham's wife for himself. He realized at once the danger he was in, and not only him but his people. *"Will you slay a nation, although blameless?"* he asks God. This illustrates something Abimelech understood about the character of God which, we, in modern times, appear to have forgotten. Something which even professing Christians need to be reminded about.

We hear talk about the personal name of God, revealed by God in the Bible as Yahweh. In former times, this was the name which was misread as Jehovah. Its various double-barrelled forms were once well known. Names such as Jehovah-jireh or "the LORD who provides." This was made famous in the story of Abraham when he was prepared to offer up his son, Isaac. Then again, Jehovah-rohi has become familiar through the 23rd psalm as "the LORD who is my shepherd", and so on. But two names which don't usually feature are Yahweh-makkeh ("the LORD who smites") and Yahweh-gemulōth ("the LORD who repays"). These two names show aspects of the character of God which the incident of Abraham's encounter with Abimelech demonstrates.

Yahweh-makkeh (Ezekiel 7:9) is "the Lord that smites," meaning he smites or strikes those who are rebellious. It's the same word "to smite" (or strike) that's found in the story of the prophet Balaam who struck his donkey when it appeared to him to be acting stubbornly in refusing to continue its journey. And it also describes God's actions against Sodom and Gomorrah; and later the land of Egypt when pharaoh, its king, refused to let God's people go in freedom. As a result, God struck the land of Egypt with the famous plagues. The other name, Yahweh-gemulōth (Jeremiah 51:56), means "the Lord who repays" and this is exactly what God did to Babylon after using them to discipline his own people's disobedience. They'd been given God's permission to take Israel captive, but they went much further in cruelty, way more than was necessary. And so they were held accountable by the God who repays. In turn, God raised up the Medo-Persian Empire and broke the power of Babylon. God 'paid back' the Babylonians for their cruelty.

These names of God, and the story of Abraham's encounter with Abimelech, reveal realities that we ignore at our peril. God is certainly gracious, and compassionate, and loving, and all

23

the things we enthusiastically commend in our preaching. But we're not faithful in the testimony we bear to God, nor to the scope of the Christian message, if we keep quiet about these other attributes of God just because they're not in sympathy with modern thought. God knows the integrity – or otherwise – of our heart in the same way as he knew the integrity of Abimelech's heart, and will repay us with what we deserve in the judgement to come unless we take advantage of his offer of a free pardon – one made possible through Christ and his sacrifice on the cross for our rebellion.

When writing about that Peter says: *"… and He Himself bore our sins in His body on the cross, so that we might die to sin and live to righteousness; for by His wounds [or "stroke"] you were healed"* (1 Peter 2:24). Actually, in the original language, the word used is the word for a single wound or stroke. This is describing Jesus on the cross bearing the punishment, the penalty from God, which we deserved, while taking our place, and as the hymnwriter says: 'That fearful stroke, it fell on Him, and life for us was won.' We're all 'dead men walking' (see Ephesians 2:1) until we realise this, and put our faith in Christ's sacrifice for us. He paid the awful price, so that believers on him may go free!

5

Jesus is Greater!

Someone hearing our title for the first time, might well ask, "greater than what?" That's totally understandable because "greater" is, after all, a comparative term. So, what are we saying Jesus is greater than? Perhaps we could give lots of answers, but Jesus himself in the twelfth chapter of Matthew's Gospel gives three specific answers, and so let's restrict ourselves to those.

We'll start by reading about the first of them. Before we do, I should say that our reading relates to an occasion in Jesus' life with his disciples when he was out for a walk with them, and without doubt it was a purposeful walk. It turns out that they weren't alone; others who weren't identified as being Jesus' disciples were observing what they were doing – and these observers included some people who were drawn from the ranks of the then religious leaders in Israel, people known as Pharisees. They were persons who tried very hard to keep strictly to the Law of Moses which originally, of course, was God-given. However these people, among others, had embellished it with lots of extra details. So, with that background, this is what Matthew records in chapter 12 ...

> *"At that time Jesus went through the grainfields on the Sabbath, and His disciples became hungry and began to pick the heads of grain and eat. But when the Pharisees saw this, they said to Him, 'Look, Your disciples do what is not lawful to do on a Sabbath.' But He said to them, 'Have you not read what David did when he became hungry, he and his companions, how he entered the house of God, and they ate the consecrated bread, which was not lawful for him to eat nor for those with him, but for the priests alone? Or have you not read in the Law, that on the Sabbath the priests in the temple break the Sabbath and are innocent? But I say to you that something greater than the temple is here'" (Matthew 12:1-6).*

Did you see that? Jesus described himself as greater than the temple. Now, it's worth pointing out that the Jews had great respect for their temple. The temple standing then in Jerusalem had been built by Jews after returning to their homeland in the 6th century B.C. King Herod had lately carried out what many judged to be improvements - doubtless it was a modernisation of sorts. So when Jesus claimed he was something greater than the temple, it must have sounded quite shocking to their ears. Basically, the temple was where people then came to connect with God. Does that help us, I wonder, to understand what Jesus is saying here when he referred to himself and declared that something greater than the temple was among them? Jesus is where we meet God. He's how we connect with God; he's the bridge, and the one and only bridge at that - the only way to God. Later, Jesus would famously declare to his disciples that no-one can come to the Father except through him (John 14:6). He, and he alone, is the way, the truth, and the life.

So, that's the first of three similar statements made by Jesus which Matthew recorded, and all of them are found in his twelfth chapter if you want to easily look them up for yourself. What we've learnt from this is that Jesus knew that the temple he spoke of would very soon be abandoned by God. Soon, a torn curtain within the temple – occurring supernaturally at the time of Jesus' death on the cross – would testify to this fact. God was no longer in residence there; he couldn't be reached by that route any more. Jesus himself, in perfect humanity and risen from the death of the cross, is declared in the Bible to be the new – and living – way to God. That makes him greater than the temple for sure. It's another encounter with the religious Pharisees that links us to the second similar statement Jesus makes in Matthew chapter 12:

"Then some of the scribes and Pharisees said to Him, 'Teacher, we want to see a sign from You.' But He answered and said to them, 'An evil and adulterous generation craves for a sign; and yet no sign will be given to it but the sign of Jonah the prophet; for just as JONAH WAS THREE DAYS AND THREE NIGHTS IN THE BELLY OF THE SEA MONSTER, so will the Son of Man be three days and three nights in the heart of the earth. The men of Nineveh will stand up with this generation at the judgment, and will condemn it because they repented at the preaching of Jonah; and behold, something greater than Jonah is here'" (Matthew 12:38-41).

Imagine you'd been there hearing those words with their reminder of the judgement that's to come. Imagine belonging to that condemned generation. We don't like to think of such things. Today, people try to convince themselves that God doesn't exist. They subscribe to the hopeless notion that we're here because of some freak cosmic accident. They try to say mindless matter somehow acquired a mind of its own – even though all our experience and knowledge shows that it doesn't make any sense to think that way. It's pure escapism. Make believe. But that's the faithlessness of our generation. Jesus compared the faithless generation of his time rather unfavourably with the brutal pagan enemy of Israel some six centuries before. At least they'd turned from their depravity to respect the true God of heaven, their creator. But it was so different with these privileged Israelites who were talking to Jesus and to whom Jesus had spoken about Jonah.

Six centuries before, the preaching of that one man, Jonah, had made a massive impact, with 120,000 lives being spared the awful doom which had been predicted. For sure, Jonah was a prophet of doom. He wasn't a compassionate man. He didn't waste any pity on his audience - they were his people's national enemy after all. He'd actually have preferred to see them burn. God had finally to take him aside and correct his attitude. The people in Jesus' day, on the other hand, had something greater - a prophet better than Jonah living among them- because Jesus' message was as much about compassion as it was about judgement. He'd come to save and not condemn; but despite that there was no massive reaction to Jesus' preaching – as there had been to Jonah's - at least not before his death. If, as we've seen earlier, Jesus is where we meet God, he's also where we encounter God's mercy.

And lastly, we come to the third and last announcement Jesus made which Matthew records like the others in his twelfth chapter. This one follows on in the same vein as the last one. Jesus now added: *"The Queen of the South will rise up with this generation at the judgment and will condemn it, because she came from the ends of the earth to hear the wisdom of Solomon; and behold, something greater than Solomon is here"* (Matthew 12:42). Earlier in the Bible, we read about the time when this took place - when the Queen of Sheba satisfied her curiosity by visiting king Solomon at Jerusalem and was overwhelmed and so impressed by all she saw and heard. She was in awe of the great wisdom God had given Solomon. In fact, she said the reports had not done it justice. Solomon had been able to answer all her questions, but the sad thing was these religious leaders were not at all impressed with Jesus – who could here claim to be something greater and better than Solomon. They came to him with their questions, some sincere but many of them trick questions to trip him up in his answers. But, of course, they never could. Jesus' answers did not satisfy idle curiosity, but exposed the intentions of the questioner's heart.

It remains true that in Jesus we have answers to life's urgent questions. What are the basic, urgent questions of this and every age? They're about life's origin and meaning, and they deal with the heavy issues of morality and destiny. Discover for yourself that in him everything was not only created but holds together. Find out for yourself that in him all the treasures of wisdom and knowledge are hidden. He's God's standard of righteousness, and - what's more - your future is in his hands.

What's the proof that Jesus is 'something better'? It's his death, burial and resurrection over the 3 days we call 'Easter.' Just as Jesus is the Bible's central figure, those 3 days are the most important of his life – essential to all the claims he makes. Jesus' dying and rising again was so that through it we can meet God, experience compassion and find truly satisfying answers in the person of God's son, who is Jesus. Don't you want "something better" in your life? Something or someone greater than the mere religious rules and rituals associated with a historic Temple. Something or someone greater than the stark doomsday predictions of a Jonah. Something greater or deeper than the theological answers of someone as wise as Solomon. Then find it in the man who died and rose at Easter-time.

6

Four Mothers

Something we all have in common is what we owe our respective mothers. Many people would lavish praise on their mother's nurturing role, sometimes expressing that in the subjective opinion that they're the world's best, etc. Sadly, there are exceptions to this where for some reason the relationship has gone disastrously wrong. I would like to speak with you about four particular mothers – they're mothers from whom we can all learn. The first I want to introduce to you is a mother who spoke about "sin." She's Susanna Wesley. You may guess from her surname that she's related to John. John Wesley's mother, Susanna, was an extraordinary woman!

As a young man, Wesley (the founder of the Methodist Church) once asked his mother for a definition of sin. She said in a letter she wrote to him on June 8, 1725: "Take this rule: whatever weakens your reason, impairs the tenderness of your conscience, obscures your sense of God, or takes off your relish of spiritual things; in short, whatever increases the strength and authority of your body over your mind, that thing is sin to you, however innocent it may be in itself." What a thoughtful answer! I would say that's entirely consistent with what the Bible says in defining for us what sin is. Romans 3:23 describes sin as a falling short of the glory of God. That's the target, the goal of human experience - we're meant to arrive at the glory of God. When we don't, we sin. Sin is therefore missing the mark or purpose for which God created humanity. From the earliest pages of the Bible, and affirmed in the New Testament, we read that we humans were created in God's image and so were meant to be the glory of God. But what does it really mean to be the glory of God?

I suggest we might think of it in this way. Just as a masterpiece of a painting might be said to be an artist's glory – because people admire it and so honour the artist who created it – so we were intended to be the crowning glory of all God's handiwork, his creation. But look what's happened. Do people tend to look at us and then be filled with admiration for God? Do any give praise and honour to the Creator because of us? That only shows how far we've fallen short, and by how much we've missed the mark. In Bible language this means we've sinned. I'm emphasizing this because it's not the common (mis)perception of sin that's around in society these days. This true definition of sin is not a definition that's conveniently narrowed down to avoidable behaviours like gross immorality or criminal activity, but is certainly something which catches us all out. And that much was certainly conveyed by Susanna Wesley's thoughtful answer. When the verb is to sin, the subject of the verb is every single one of us at some time or other – and very much more often than we might suspect.

Susanna Wesley had a sense of God, and the more sense of God we have then the more conscious we'll be of sin in our lives. Those who talk today about even quite blatant acts of immorality or fraudulent dealings as being only "errors of judgement" or mere "indiscretions" display their ignorance of God and the almost total lack of respect for him in their lives no matter how high a standing they have in public office. So, sin in the Bible's terms is a failure to reach the mark, and how disappointing it is to be conscious of the fact that we're not achieving what we were designed to be and do in our role as the image and glory of God. Yes, failure and disappointment are inherent in the human condition as we find it now. So much so, that we must ask the question: "Is there any hope – or is it hopeless?"

At this point, I'd like to introduce another mother. This time, it's the mother of Jesus Christ. Let's think of the time when she saw the Saviour, her son, dying on the cross being crucified by the Roman soldiers at Pilate's command. One man has employed his imagination in an appealing way, I think, and written this simple verse of poetry:

> Her face showed grief, but not despair
> Her head though bowed had faith to spare.
> And even now she could suppose
> His thorns would somehow yield a rose.
> Her life with Him was full of signs
> That God writes straight with crooked lines.
> Dark clouds can hide the rising sun
> And all seem lost when all be won.

The author of those lines was a man going through a terrible time, a time which had evidently caused him to reflect seriously on the cross of Christ and the great sacrifice our Lord made for all of us there. He shared much of his gruesome experiences in a book entitled *When Hell Was In Session.* The author was Jeremiah Denton, who subsequently rose to the rank of rear admiral in the US Navy. In November 1980, Denton became the first retired flag officer ever elected to the U.S. Senate. In 1987, he was appointed by President Ronald Reagan to be Chairman of the Presidential Commission on Merchant Marine and Defense.

But back in 1973 Jeremiah Denton walked to freedom after being held captive in North Vietnam for more than seven years. He'd been captured in July 1965 after leading a bombing attack on enemy installations where he'd been shot down and captured by North Vietnamese troops. While held prisoner Denton became the first American subjected to four years of solitary confinement. In 1966, during a television interview by the North Vietnamese broadcast on American television Denton gained national attention when while being questioned he blinked his eyes in Morse code, repeatedly spelling out the covert message "T-O-R-T-U-R-E."

At times, life's experiences deepen mere disappointment into utter despair. We struggle to remember Betsy Ten Boom's words at the height of her own war-time sufferings: "There's no pit so deep but God's love isn't deeper still." Denton had penned that poem about his felt sense of hopelessness – the poem we quoted above – when taking inspiration and courage from the thought of Mary looking at Jesus on the cross.

Her face showed grief, but not despair
Her head though bowed had faith to spare.

> And even now she could suppose
> His thorns would somehow yield a rose.
> Her life with Him was full of signs
> That God writes straight with crooked lines.
> Dark clouds can hide the rising sun
> And all seem lost when all be won.

Evidently, this helped him travel from hopelessness and disappointment back to hope again. It's only by looking to the cross, as he pictured Mary doing, that any of us can find true reason to hope. We need to look to the cross of Jesus in faith.

So let's conclude with a couple of mothers whose lives evidenced genuine faith. That was the verdict of the Apostle Paul when he wrote to Timothy saying: *"I have been reminded of your sincere faith, which first lived in your grandmother Lois and in your mother Eunice and, I am persuaded, now lives in you also."* Like them, to come into the full experience of God's love - to be sure of God's forgiveness with all our guilt removed - we need to profess faith in the one God sent: Jesus. On four occasions the Bible tells us *"whoever believes in him* [that's Jesus] *will not be disappointed"* (Isaiah 28:16; Romans 9:33; Romans 10:11; 1 Peter 2:6). This is the only complete antidote to disappointment that sinners can ever find. He or she who believes in Jesus will not be disappointed in any ultimate sense.

Our four featured mothers have impressed on us sensitivity to the ways of God, then also strength of character in being able to express hope in the face of adversity, and finally genuine faith which may even impact the rising generations among us. These are all things which are vital. We do need to be sensitive

35

to our failure through sin (even for the best of us, God's original intention can no longer be realized in the way we are now); but we also need to be open to the hope for the hopeless that's available through the cross of Christ. Finally, we must access that hope by applying for its benefit through faith. Will you do that?

7

Death-bed Conversations

We talk about people wanting to have the last word. But I don't suppose there are many, if any, who want the words they've just spoken to be the last they'll ever utter. During evangelistic crusades held in London in 1883 and 1884, renowned preacher D. L. Moody once threw down the gauntlet to all the atheist clubs there, challenging their members to come to a special service to be held exclusively for them. Thousands came, curious perhaps, but certainly determined to make a fool of this upstart American preacher.

Once in the pulpit, Moody preached from the Bible verse found in Deuteronomy 32:31 – *"Their rock is not as our Rock, even our enemies themselves being judges."* He then proceeded to tell story after story from his repertoire of bedside conversations with dying men and women, both believers and unbelievers. He spoke with compassion and devastating effect to a full hall, and called on his sceptical audience to judge for themselves between the death-bed statements of believers and the death-bed statements of unbelievers as to whose 'rock' was the best.

As he continued preaching, God broke through in these free-thinking hearts, and from that night until the end of the week, about 2000 atheists were drawn to the Saviour, who is Jesus Christ.

If we were to do something similar to what Moody did then, we'd tell of the 18th century French Enlightenment writer, Voltaire, who cried out in death "I am abandoned by God and man." His nurse, who was witness to his torment, said she never wanted to see another infidel die – not for all the wealth of Europe. Voltaire, one of history's best-known atheists, often stated that "by the time I'm buried, the Bible will be non-existent." His actual last words were: "I am abandoned by God and man; I shall die and go to hell alone." His condition had become so terrible that his associates were afraid to approach his bedside as he passed away. A few years after he died, it's reported that the Geneva Bible Society purchased Voltaire's home and turned it into a print shop to print Bibles – so much for him saying the Bible wouldn't even exist then!

Sir Walter Raleigh (1554 – 1618) was an English aristocrat, a writer, poet, soldier, courtier, spy, and explorer – one especially well known for making tobacco popular in England. He was a favourite of Queen Elizabeth, but greatly disliked by her successor, James the First, who ordered his execution. When the time came, the executioner was advising him how best to place his head, when Raleigh replied "It matters little how the head lies, my friend, so long as the heart is right." And so ended one of the more colourful characters of the Elizabethan era.

Speaking of which, Elizabeth I (1533 – 1603) was the last

monarch of the Tudor dynasty, being the daughter of Henry VIII. Dying, she famously said: "All my possessions for a moment of time." But that's one thing money can't buy. One report says she grabbed the sleeve of her physician and pulled him down over her bed and said: "Half of the British Empire for six months of life." He could not even give her six minutes, and she died. I also found these words about Stalin's deathbed scene, as related by his daughter Svetlana to Malcolm Muggeridge. This was Stalin who murdered millions of his own countrymen. While on his deathbed, he "suddenly sat up ... shook his fist at the ceiling as if he could see beyond it, then fell back and died." He'd denied God's existence, and so you have to ask: "Against whom was he shaking his fist when he came to die?" That reminds me of Julian the Apostate, who was a Roman emperor who hated Christians, and was leading his forces in the battle for Persia in 363 AD. He was mortally wounded, and as he lay dying on the battlefield he picked up some of his own blood, mingled it with dirt, then flung it skyward and said: "You have conquered, O Galilean!" (that being a reference to Jesus, of course).

Michael Faraday, (1791 – 1867) was an English scientist of whom another scientist, Rutherford, stated: "When we consider the magnitude and extent of his discoveries and their influence on the progress of science and of industry, there is no honour too great to pay to the memory of Faraday, one of the greatest scientific discoverers of all time." This great man Faraday was asked when he was near death: "What are your speculations now?" He answered: "I have no speculations. I rest upon Jesus Christ who died, and rose again from death." Contrast that with the case of Thomas Hobbes - 17th century English philosopher – who said famously when on his death-bed: "Now am I about to take my last voyage - a great leap in the dark." Sir Walter Scott the sceptic said: "Until this moment I thought there was neither a God nor a hell. Now I know that there are both, and I am doomed to perdition by the just judgment of the Almighty."

United States' President George Washington said at the end of his life: "Doctor, I am dying, but I am not afraid to die." He then folded his hands over his chest and said: "It is well." Michelangelo, the famous painter and sculptor said at the end of his life: "I die in the faith of Jesus Christ, and in the firm hope of a better life." The final words of David Brainerd, (a well-known missionary) were: "I am going into eternity and it is sweet to me to think of eternity." Talleyrand, someone who has been called the most brilliant mind of his generation, when asked about his condition while on his deathbed, replied: "I am suffering the pangs of the damned." William Pitt, the renowned British statesman, just before he died said: "I throw myself on the mercy of God, through the merits of Jesus Christ." Charles Haddon Spurgeon, famous preacher and author, on his deathbed, said: "I can hear them coming!" He sat straight up in bed and asked: "Don't you hear them? This is my coronation day. I can see the chariots, and I'm ready to board."

Dietrich Bonhoffer, German theologian, standing in front of a firing squad during World War 2, for speaking out against Nazism, "This may seem to be the end for me, but it is just the beginning." Sir Julian Huxley, English evolutionist, biologist and staunch atheist, on his deathbed said: "So it is true after all, so it is true after all." P. T. Barnum the circus magnate on his deathbed asked: "How are the circus receipts today?" Cesare Borgia, a famous writer and politician was a meticulous planner. He planned everything to the minutest detail. When he knew he was dying said: "When I lived I provided for everything, except death. Now I must die, and I am totally unprepared and unprovided." Adams, the infidel upon dying said: "I'm lost, lost, lost. I am damned forever." His agony was so great that as he died, he tore the hair from his head.

And what of the American preacher, D.L. Moody, who set us off on this train of thought? While on his deathbed, he asked: "Can this be death? Why it is better than living! Earth is receding, heaven is opening. This is my coronation day." I think you will agree, that it's safe to conclude there's a very great difference between the last words of believers and unbelievers. Let unbelievers with their final words be our judges. *"Their rock is not as our Rock, even our enemies themselves being judges"* (Deuteronomy 32:31).

8

The Lever of the Gospel

Leading the siege of Syracuse was a Roman general Marcus Claudius Marcellus, whose nickname was 'The Sword of Rome.' When Marcellus brought his troops and the Roman navy up against the citadel of Syracuse, the Romans encountered war machines the like of which they'd never seen. These were weapons of destruction far more sophisticated than anything which the Romans themselves had ever invented. Now, one of those war machines was as astonishing as it was terrifying to the Roman navy, for as their ships approached the cliffs outside Syracuse, the sailors looked up and saw huge jaws descending from the sky. These jaws came down, and would grip a Roman ship, hoist it a hundred feet into the air, and then release it so that ship and crew were dashed against the rocks. The Romans couldn't believe their eyes when they saw such ropes and metal being manipulated by these new technical marvels of pulleys and levers.

Eventually, however, the Romans were victorious. And General Marcellus gave the command that the engineer who'd developed these new weapons was to be unharmed, when and if he was found. But as a Roman soldier approached the engineer as he was sitting with other prisoners; he found him passing the time by doing mathematical equations in the sand. The man was so absorbed in calculation that he didn't notice it was a Roman soldier who was approaching him. Without taking his eyes off his calculations in the sand he said, *"Be careful! Don't disturb my diagrams!"* And the Roman soldier killed him on the spot. And thus *Archimedes* met his death ...

Greek by birth, born in 287 BC in Syracuse to Greek parents, educated in Alexandria, Egypt, Archimedes went on to become a remarkable mathematician, an exacting engineer, a brilliant inventor, a master craftsman, a skilful builder, and something of a philosopher. It was the same Archimedes who, after figuring out the laws of buoyancy while stepping into his bathtub, ran straight out into the streets naked shouting "Eureka! (I've found it!)." Archimedes defined the principle of the lever, and is credited with inventing the pulley. We're talking about one of the most brilliant men of all time. You may have heard of the words he spoke to the king of Syracuse on one occasion: *"Give me a lever long enough, and a place to stand, and I will move the whole world."* A little over two hundred years after Archimedes made that statement a lever *was* indeed found that could move the world. Revealed in the Gospel of the cross of Christ is the power of God which alone is able to right a topsy-turvy world. It was the message of the cross, which created the necessary leverage that continues to change the world.

In Acts 17:6 we read, *"These men who have turned the world upside down ..."* when referring to Paul and Silas who used that same

Gospel lever to turn the ancient world upside down. By the way, when the Bible speaks of turning the world upside down, as we said already, it's really speaking in terms of turning the world the *right side up.* For we live in a topsy-turvy world, a world where all around us the wicked prosper, and the righteous suffer; where sin is often exalted, and virtue mocked; a world in which it's been said that *"Beggars ride on horseback while princes walk in rags."* Ever since Eden, this world has been the wrong way up. And the message of Christianity is about what God has done, through the cross of Christ, to turn the world the right way up again. Let's let the Apostle Paul in the Bible expand on the revolutionary, or counter-cultural, ideas of the Christian message.

> *"For the word of the cross is foolishness to those who are perishing, but to us who are being saved it is the power of God. For it is written, 'I WILL DESTROY THE WISDOM OF THE WISE, AND THE CLEVERNESS OF THE CLEVER I WILL SET ASIDE.' Where is the wise man? Where is the scribe? Where is the debater of this age? Has not God made foolish the wisdom of the world? For since in the wisdom of God the world through its wisdom did not come to know God, God was well-pleased through the foolishness of the message preached to save those who believe. For indeed Jews ask for signs and Greeks search for wisdom; but we preach Christ crucified, to Jews a stumbling block and to Gentiles foolishness, but to those who are the called, both Jews and Greeks, Christ the power of God and the wisdom of God"* (1 Corinthians 1:18-24).

You'll have noticed the upside-down character of the Christian message as Paul expands on it there. The world's wisdom is poles apart from God's wisdom; and at the centre of the conflict stands the cross of Christ. The world's verdict on Christ stands recorded at the cross. And by the verdict which it decidedly expressed there – when they said "away with him" – this world stands judged before God. Because through the apparent folly of a man dying a criminal's death, God has revealed real wisdom and power which are for the forgiveness from guilt of all who believe. Paul continues on this theme of the Gospel into the next chapter, into 1 Corinthians chapter 2, so let's take it a bit further:

> *"And when I came to you, brethren, I did not come with superiority of speech or of wisdom, proclaiming to you the testimony of God. For I determined to know nothing among you except Jesus Christ, and Him crucified. I was with you in weakness and in fear and in much trembling, and my message and my preaching were not in persuasive words of wisdom, but in demonstration of the Spirit and of power"* (1 Corinthians 2:1-4).

Let me just pause again there. Paul's just talked about the testimony of God; the cross of Christ; and the power of the Spirit. God the Father, Son and Spirit are involved in giving this message its great leverage through the cross: giving it its power to move the world and overturn human opinion. But we'll let Paul say a bit more ...

> *"... so that your faith would not rest on the wisdom of men, but on the power of God. Yet we do speak wisdom among those who are mature; a wisdom, however, not of this age nor of the rulers of this age, who are passing away;*

*but we speak God's wisdom in a mystery, the hidden
wisdom which God predestined before the ages to our
glory; the wisdom which none of the rulers of this age
has understood; for if they had understood it they would
not have crucified the Lord of glory ..."* (1 Corinthians
2:5-8).

We talked a moment ago about toppling human opinion.
Heaven's view of the death of Christ (the cross) is totally
different from earth's. Like the ancient Greeks, the world
in its intellectual pride still disregards the cross as insignificant.
And like the Jews of old, the world in its religious systems of
thought has emptied the cross of its power. The Bible language
here invites us to say that God has in fact scandalized the world
at the cross, by the death of Christ his son. Attitudes to the
death of Christ expose fundamental misunderstandings of what
God has achieved through the cross. But, the cross does make
sense! Not only that, but it's the only thing that can make sense
of everything! This is the phenomenal leverage of the Christian
message of the cross. There's a deep wisdom which God reveals
here: one which plumbs the depths of God and eternity, which
is why Paul now says ...

*"... but just as it is written, 'THINGS WHICH EYE HAS
NOT SEEN AND EAR HAS NOT HEARD, AND which HAVE
NOT ENTERED THE HEART OF MAN, ALL THAT GOD HAS
PREPARED FOR THOSE WHO LOVE HIM.' For to us God
revealed them through the Spirit; for the Spirit searches
all things, even the depths of God. For who among men
knows the thoughts of a man except the spirit of the man
which is in him? Even so the thoughts of God no one*

46

knows except the Spirit of God. Now we have received,
not the spirit of the world, but the Spirit who is from God,
so that we may know the things freely given to us by God"
(1 Corinthians 2:9-12).

The Roman navy saw things they'd never seen before at Syracuse when they came up against Archimedes' levers and pulleys. When God's Spirit gives you biblical insight into the meaning of Christ's death as it stands for ever at the centre of God's purposes for the human race (and beyond), you, too, will see undreamt of things. There's such a depth to the meaning of the cross that the most brilliant academic mind and the most impressive oratory won't even scratch the surface – indeed they'll miss the mark completely. If I can't read even your thoughts, how can I - or you - read God's thoughts? And we need to do precisely that if we're to appreciate the cross of Christ. That's why the preaching of the Christian message in its power to change and bring leverage depends vitally on the operation of God's Spirit: with the person of the Holy Spirit communicating through the preacher.

Angels, we're told have a great desire to research this topic, but even they don't get very far. To share the depths of God, we need the help of someone who is God – the Holy Spirit. He's been speaking and preaching about the cross for a very long time indeed, previously using the Old Testament prophets. But in those earlier times God wasn't permitting a clear advance understanding. He is now. The truth is out. Those who are of the world can't receive this, only those who belong to God, all who are on the side of truth. Now, is that you?

9

From Pearl Harbour to the Pearly Gates

Mitsuo Fuchida grew up loving his native Japan and hating the United States, which treated Asian immigrants harshly in the first half of the twentieth century. Fuchida attended a military academy, joined Japan's Naval Air Force, and by 1941, with 10,000 flying hours behind him, had become established as the nation's top pilot. And so, when Japanese military leaders needed someone to command a surprise attack on Pearl Harbour, they chose Fuchida. His was the voice that sent his aircraft carrier the message "Tora! Tora! Tora! (Tiger! Tiger! Tiger!)" indicating the success of the mission.

The attack on Pearl Harbour was a surprise military strike conducted by the Imperial Japanese Navy against the United States naval base at Pearl Harbour, in Hawaii, on the morning of December 7, 1941 (December 8 in Japan). The attack was intended to warn the U.S. Pacific Fleet against interfering with any military actions the Empire of Japan was planning. The Pearl Harbour base was attacked by 353 Japanese fighters, bombers and torpedo planes in two waves, launched from six aircraft carriers. All eight U.S. Navy battleships were damaged, with four being sunk. The attack came as a profound shock to the American people and led directly to the American entry into World War II. The following day (December 8), the United States declared war on Japan. Domestic support for non-interventionism, which had been strong in the US, had all but disappeared overnight.

Jacob DeShazer was a young American serviceman. He was peeling potatoes at his army base in California when he heard about the Pearl Harbour attack. The Japanese air force had struck without warning against US Navy ships in harbour at Hawaii. DeShazer's first impulse was to throw a potato against the wall and shout for revenge. The news hit him so hard that it seemed as if he instantly and passionately hated the Japanese people for their treacherous and devastating attack. DeShazer got his chance of revenge. He took part in the surprise retaliatory air raid on Tokyo. He went as a bombardier. However, things didn't go to plan. The plane he was in ran out of fuel. He and others had to parachute down somewhere in China. Some vanished forever in the mountains, but DeShazer was captured by the Japanese. The Japanese prison into which DeShazer and the other American POWS were thrown was a brutal place, where torture was added to the starvation. Formerly strong-muscled men were reduced to pitiful, living skeletons. DeShazer watched helplessly as his room-mate died from the effects of starvation and as a result of a fatal heart attack.

By 1945, Fuchida had attained the position of the Imperial Navy's Air Operations Officer. On August 6 he was eating breakfast in Nara, Japan, where a new military headquarters was under construction, when he heard about a bomb dropped on Hiroshima. He flew to investigate, then sent a grim report to the Imperial Command. On the same day, Jacob DeShazer had felt prompted by the Holy Spirit, he would later claim, to pray for peace. He'd been in captivity since 1942, when, after dropping his bombs near Tokyo, he'd been forced to parachute into China. While imprisoned, first in Nanjing and later in Beijing, DeShazer had become a Christian. He'd been reading First Corinthians chapter 13, the Bible's great chapter on love, the one so often read at weddings. Reading this, in these circumstances, had transformed him. Jacob DeShazer's almost insane hatred for the torturing Japanese prison guards was replaced with love, the kind of love he'd been reading about from the pages of the Bible.

He found his heart softened toward his Japanese captors. After being liberated, DeShazer wrote a widely distributed essay, "*I Was a Prisoner of the Japanese,*" detailing his experiences of capture, conversion, and forgiveness. He'd returned to the United States and gone to Seattle Pacific College, but he began to feel the urge to quit studying and go back to Japan to share the good news of the Christian faith.

Meanwhile, after the war, Mitsuo Fuchida, the Pearl Harbour attack squadron commander, now bitter over Japan's humiliating defeat and unconditional surrender, left professional army life and returned to his family farm and settled for a life of menial drudgery. All the while, he'd later say, his soul was churning with misery and torment over a once highly successful life in the military that'd gone nowhere.

Let's switch back once again and catch up with DeShazer. By

now he was convinced he'd been called by the Lord to go back to Japan with the Gospel, so DeShazer dropped his studies and obeyed. One day he was sharing his life story in that essay of his – now a pamphlet, but with the same title: "*I was a Prisoner of War.*" He was standing at the busy Shibuya train station in Tokyo. And guess who should come along? Yes, Mitsuo Fuchida, the commander of the Pearl Harbour attack squadron, passed by – the commander of the Pearl Harbour fighter planes that took over two thousand American lives!

He'd been back to Tokyo to testify at one of the hearings held by General MacArthur concerning Japanese war crimes. Mitsuo received one of the pamphlets Jacob DeShazer was handing out to passers-by. Of course, DeShazer didn't know Mitsuo Fuchida by sight – he'd only heard of him. Then Fuchida and DeShazer actually met in 1950. Fuchida told DeShazer how he'd read his pamphlet, bought a Bible, and then converted from Buddhism to Christianity. The irresistible power of Christ's love in Jacob DeShazer's story had transformed him into a believer in Jesus Christ. DeShazer had just finished a 40-day fast for revival in Japan at the time when Fuchida came to his home and introduced himself. DeShazer welcomed the new convert and encouraged him to be baptized. While DeShazer continued to plant churches throughout Japan, Fuchida became an evangelist, spreading a message of peace and forgiveness in his native country and throughout Asian-American communities.

Fuchida died on May 30, 1976. He wrote, "That morning [of the attack on Pearl Harbour] ... I lifted the curtain of warfare by dispatching that cursed order, and I put my whole effort into the war that followed. ... [But] after buying and reading the

Bible, my mind was strongly impressed and captivated. I think I can say today without hesitation that God's grace has been set upon me." As I think of these two men, one American and the other Japanese, men who'd been conditioned to hate one another, and to regard each other as enemies, but who each through the transforming power of the Christian message had been reconciled first to God and also to each other, it seems right to borrow and apply Bible words which in their original setting apply to the hostility between Jew and Gentile: *"But now in Christ Jesus you who formerly were far off have been brought near by the blood of Christ. For He Himself is our peace, who made both groups into one and broke down the barrier of the dividing wall"* (Ephesians 2:13-14).

Joseph DeShazer and Mitsuo Fuchida – men whose lives on earth were brought together by Pearl Harbour, will for ever – based on their credible testimony – have an association with the Pearl Gates of the city the Apostle John describes at the end of the Bible – and with these words we'll conclude …

> *"And I saw the holy city, new Jerusalem, coming down out of heaven from God, made ready as a bride adorned for her husband …. and He will wipe away every tear from their eyes; and there will no longer be any death; there will no longer be any mourning, or crying, or pain; the first things have passed away … And the twelve gates were twelve pearls; each one of the gates was a single pearl. And the street of the city was pure gold, like transparent glass"* (Revelation 21:2,4,21).

10

The Shame of Being Known

Some cultures are described as guilt cultures; whereas others are spoken of as shame cultures. In either kind of culture, if I believe I'm guilty, AND society believes I'm guilty, then I'm in big trouble, and I'll be punished. On the other hand, if I believe I'm not guilty AND so does society, then there's no problem. Where it gets interesting is when I believe something different about myself from what society thinks of me – or more to the point perhaps, their view of me is different from how I view myself. Let's suppose I live in a guilt culture, and society doesn't believe I'm guilty but I believe I'm guilty. In that case, I can't live with myself. In a guilt culture it's what I believe about myself that controls my response. I can't cope with believing I'm guilty - irrespective of what others believe about me. Sometimes, someone who's been found not guilty in a court of law, will later – quite voluntarily – make a confession to the police that they really did commit the crime that they were previously accused of. They just couldn't live with the personal knowledge of their guilt.

But it's the opposite way round in a shame culture. There, it doesn't matter if I believe in my innocence, because as long as society believes I'm guilty, I simply can't live with the shame that brings. In a shame culture, it's what society believes about me that's controls my response. I can't cope with the shame of them thinking I'm guilty - irrespective of whether I am or not. Sometimes, in such a culture, the mere shameful suspicion of others thinking that a person is guity is sufficient for that person to feel like life is no longer worth living.

At a purely personal level, as opposed to the cultural level, I think we can all relate to that last idea. We're all concerned about what others know and think about us. That's why we have secrets AND yet - at the same time - feel a need to share them in a controlled way. A few years ago, one man had an idea. He decided to start a blog—intended to be a temporary community art project—in which individuals would mail postcards on which was written just one secret which they hadn't told to anyone. This blog is now an online community with over 80,000 members. Those with secrets seem to feel the need to tell them to somebody but only in a safe or controlled way because being truly known outside of that brings fear. Being known opens us up to exposure, and if we're exposed we risk being rejected. Normally, we prefer to keep hidden from others whatever shameful secrets lurk in the dark recesses of our souls. We hide our secrets and put on our public face hoping that what we really are will never be seen or known by anyone else. But even deeper down, secure behind the protection of anonymity perhaps, we also long for the relief of unburdening.

Given this fear of being known, the invitation "Come, see a

man who told me all the things that I have done," might've been heard more like an accusation than an invitation. Yet, this invitation—given by an unnamed, Samaritan woman in the fourth chapter of John's Gospel —is an invitation to see, and to be seen by someone who's told her all that she'd done. That someone was Jesus. Now, his knowledge didn't reject or destroy this relationship. The knowledge of her which Jesus demonstrated had obviously restored her sense of worth – judging by her elated response.

We're only given a few details about this woman. She was a Samaritan, a long-despised ethnic group. We're told that she'd had five husbands and was currently living with a man to whom she wasn't married. It could well be that this is the source of her shame. Women in the ancient world derived their social standing as well as their economic viability from their husbands. With neither husband nor male child, a woman such as this was dependent on a society that often abandoned them. It's often thought this woman was coming to draw water when no other women were around so that she could hide her shame. This is because it's reckoned unlikely that she'd outlived five men; more likely that they'd chosen to use her and then abandon her. In that place where she lived, hers is an open secret but still one that's too painful to sit comfortably with out in the open. Yet in her brief encounter with a stranger who asks her to give him a drink, her secrets are exposed. But not for the sake of shaming her or exposing what she feared the most. The stranger by the well at no point invites repentance nor, for that matter, does he speak of sin at all. That would indicate to me that this woman already had the right attitude towards her past life.

"Sir, I can see you are a prophet," she said – which is interesting, because Jesus hadn't told her future – which is the thing many would equate with prophecy. In fact, he'd actually told her past. *"You are right when you say you have no husband. The fact is, you have had five husbands, and the man you now have is not your husband"* (John 4:17-18). From his knowledge of her shameful personal life, the woman at the well concluded that Jesus was nothing less than a prophet. As the conversation continued, she began to wonder if Jesus wasn't in fact more than just any prophet, but the very one the Old Testament promised. We said it's immediately after Jesus describes her past that she says, *"I see that you are a prophet."* She *sees* because Jesus has *seen* her - seen her past pain. He's seen her including her shameful secret, but offered her something of incomparable worth: namely his acceptance of her, all bound up in the offer of living water. He has *seen* her—and, boy, was she thirsty for the worth, value and significance that are available from him.

All of this is treatment that she's unaccustomed to receive – from anyone. Perhaps she'd given up expecting it from any female, far less a man. Never mind the fact that this man is a Jew and not one of her own Samaritan people! Racial and cultural taboos don't seem to matter to this man. When he speaks knowingly and compassionately of her past, she realizes she's in the presence of a prophet. She leaves her waterpot, runs into her city, and invites all the townspeople to *"come, see a man who told me all the things I have done."* *"Come, see a man who told me all the things that I have done"* becomes an invitation to be welcomed into living life in the open. Jesus knows the most intimate details of our life – both our guilt and shame and all our secrets, but from the example of her case, we see that needn't make us feel afraid or ashamed. That's because his knowledge brings a sense of worth because it conveys his acceptance.

It's interesting that before John in his Gospel tells us of the Lord's insight into this woman's past, he also records Jesus' insight into the life of two men. The first is someone called Nathaniel. We read in John 1:

> *"Philip found Nathanael and said to him, 'We have found Him of whom Moses in the Law and also the Prophets wrote—Jesus of Nazareth, the son of Joseph.' Nathanael said to him, 'Can any good thing come out of Nazareth?' Philip said to him, 'Come and see.' Jesus saw Nathanael coming to Him, and said of him, 'Behold, an Israelite indeed, in whom there is no deceit!' Nathanael said to Him, 'How do You know me?' Jesus answered and said to him, 'Before Philip called you, when you were under the fig tree, I saw you.' Nathanael answered Him, 'Rabbi, You are the Son of God; You are the King of Israel'"* (John 1:45-49).

So Jesus first revealed what was in Nathaniel's heart, and so exposed his character, and this led to the further revelation to Nathaniel that the one who could do this was their long-awaited Messiah – Philip had been right after all! This is evidence to support what we're told in the next chapter: *"But Jesus, on His part, was not entrusting Himself to them, for He knew all men, and because He did not need anyone to testify concerning man, for He Himself knew what was in man"* (John 2:24-25). Next up is a man called Nicodemus. He arrives on the scene straight after our being told that Jesus knows us and all that's in us.

"Now there was a man of the Pharisees, named Nicodemus, a ruler of the Jews; this man came to Jesus by night and said to Him, 'Rabbi, we know that You have come from God as a teacher; for no one can do these signs that You do unless God is with him.' Jesus answered and said to him, 'Truly, truly, I say to you, unless one is born again he cannot see the kingdom of God' (John 3:1-3).

At first, it seems like Jesus is answering a question that's never been asked. But, of course, this is the very matter that's been playing on Nicodemus' mind. And so the stage is set for the question about how we may be born again to be answered by one of the most well-loved of Bible verses: John 3:16 – *"For God so loved the world that he gave his one and only son that whoever believes in him will not perish but have eternal life."* By this means we can know for certain that we're no longer guilty before God because our sins are now forgiven and our worrying about being shamefully exposed is also dealt with as we, through faith, are fitted for heaven and become acceptable to God through being found in Christ by faith alone. For those in either a guilt or shame culture, this is good news indeed!

11

Four Things God Wants You to Know

"Houston, we have a problem," is a piece of United States space program jargon that's become an instantly recognisible expression well beyond the US. Many of us have been held as if spellbound viewing a live televised transmission of some daring space mission. I can recall during my final year in junior school the teacher bringing a television set into the classroom so we could watch the historic drama of the first moon-landing being played out. At times like that if those astronauts in their fragile space vessel way out in space should communicate with the space centre in Houston saying "Houston, we have a problem," then our hearts miss a beat – their lives could be hanging in the balance.

Yes, some problems can be serious. And communications at times like that can be critical. The Bible is God's communication to us, in which he tells us that we have a problem (Romans 6:23; Ephesians 2:1). Before I come to that, allow me, if you will, another reminiscence. I remember in January 2004 while I was in the Philippines, reading in the Philippine Inquirer newspaper about a moratorium on drug dealers. As a result of an appeal by the Pope their death sentence was postponed. The newspaper described those who were on death row and who were waiting for their fate to be determined as being "the living dead of the Philippines." Some newspaper headlines are very effective. That must have been one was because I've never forgotten it.

But here's the point: I've some really Good News for you, from the Bible, and it comes to you from the God who knows your name and loves you – but before you can appreciate this good news, you first need to realize that you're under a worse death sentence than those drug-dealers. As sinners in God's sight, every one born - not only in the Philippines but anywhere in the world today - is born with an eternal death sentence hanging over their head – in other words, we're all the living dead of this planet! "Dead in sins" is how the Bible in Ephesians chapter 2 begins to describe those who don't know God. Now, I'm not here to tell you about how it can be postponed, but to tell you about how God has actually made a way back to life for you – and that's a way back to experiencing life in its fullest sense for ever.

And that's because, in that same Bible chapter of Ephesians chapter 2, but this time in verses 8 & 9, there's an announcement about God's grace, which is the underserved favour he shows us. But even as the Bible here tells us about God's amazing grace towards sinners (which is all of us), it also mentions that our own good works can't save us. This is because, as we've seen, we're actually dead in God's sight – because of our sins. That's why we can't even begin to hope that God will be pleased by our good works and let us into heaven. Please allow me to illustrate how many people think, so that we can realize for ourselves how utterly hopeless this kind of thinking is. Let's imagine again a dispute between neighbours which comes before a local magistrate. One man is accused of stealing his neighbour's motorbike. This is what he says to the magistrate: "I am here today to demand justice. I don't want mercy or compassion, I simply want justice. In connection with the theft of the motorbike which I'm being accused of, I admit that I did it. But there have been many other days when I did not steal his motorbike. I have even done some good things for him on a few occasions. So, on that basis, I demand justice. I demand to be declared innocent and free to go!" Now, let me ask you, what do you think the magistrate will say? Will he be convinced by this argument? No, of course not! And neither will God be if we plead that our good works should cancel out our sins. But I'm here to tell you positively, that there's a way back to life with God and Calvary's cross where Jesus, God's Son, died for you, is the place where you begin.

It was there where Jesus died that God solved our problem for us (1 Corinthians 15:3,4). What's more, Jesus came back from the dead to be our risen, living Saviour. Please allow me to tell you a recent story of how – in another sense – a person came back to life. In 1997, the house Luz lived in was badly damaged by fire. This, it was suspected, was due to a faulty power cable. Her daughter Delimar's bedroom was so totally destroyed by the intense heat that no trace of Delimar's dead body was ever found. Later, 6 years later in fact, Luz was attending a party where a 6 year old girl was present. Instantly and impossibly, but with a mother's intuition, she knew she was looking at her very own daughter. She pretended there was gum stuck to her hair and cut out a few strands for DNA testing which confirmed this was indeed her daughter! What had happened was that someone known to the family, a person called Carolyn Correa, had visited just after baby Delimar's birth claiming she was pregnant. Police believe she snatched the child and then set fire to the baby's bedroom to cover up her kidnap. Still more amazingly, Jesus in reality came back from the dead physically, so we can come back from the dead spiritually. He is God's provision for our problem, the problem we're unable to fix on our own.

So, you may say, what exactly am I supposed to do? Well, this is how we must now respond – I want to use a story Jesus himself told in Luke 15:17-21. We're asking: How does Jesus' death on the cross come to save us? We need to hear again the moral of the story of the prodigal son which Jesus told in Luke 15 – it's all about the boy who took his father's money and ran away from home. Later, he was sorry and came back. The father, when welcoming him home again, said about his son that it was as if he was alive again. Now, let me tell you this, God is like that father; but in order for things to be right again between us and God, we must come back to God the very same way that prodigal returned to his father – in other words, by not boasting about the good works we like to remember, but by admitting our bad deeds, the ones we'd prefer to forget.

The prodigal did this after the Bible says he "came to himself" – in other words after he came to his senses. You can read in Luke's Gospel how his father "had compassion" – which confirms the boy was in big trouble from every point of view. Then, finally, the son admitted: "I'm not worthy." May I ask if you spoken to God like that? That's the true way to come back to God as if from the dead – turning your life round to find the way to life. The father said of his boy that it was as if he'd been dead and was now alive again.

We've by now made it clear, I hope, that we're not good enough for heaven, but in case anyone here thinks the opposite - that they're too bad for heaven, let me tell you about a young girl on a plane who was obviously travelling to visit her dad. Let me describe her to you: she's in a pretty dress with pink ribbons in her hair and black shiny shoes. All the time she's singing loudly "I'm going to see daddy ..." Every chance she gets while on the plane she has a Pepsi and a cake. She keeps bouncing up and down with excitement, until well ... you can guess what happened. She exploded. I mean she was violently sick. Now the little girl with pink ribbons in her hair and nice dress and black shiny shoes was in a terrible mess. When people got out of the plane as soon as it landed, escaping in a hurry from the mess and smell, they were interested to see a man in a light-coloured suit of immaculate clothes heading for the plane – surely, this was her dad coming to meet his daughter. How was he going to react, when he saw the disgusting mess she was in now?

The little girl saw him and rushed towards him. In a split second, he saw the terrible mess she was in ... but he didn't hesitate – he stretched out his arms and hugged her close. And that's how God in his grace welcomes us, as in fact the farmer did his rebel boy. There's no life that's too messed up. God wants to welcome you back – as someone who was effectively dead to him, but who's alive again. Yes, today, right where you are, you can find your way back to life with God through Jesus' death and all by God's grace. According to John 5:24 just by hearing and believing you can pass in a moment from death to life. This is Good News for all, for everyone, but you must come on your own, when you come to God through Jesus.

About the Author

Born and educated in Scotland, Brian worked as a government scientist until God called him into full-time Christian ministry on behalf of the Churches of God (www.churchesofgod.info). His voice has been heard on Search For Truth radio broadcasts for over 40 years (visit www.searchfortruth.podbean.com) during which time he has been an itinerant Bible teacher throughout the UK. His evangelical and missionary work outside the UK is primarily in Belgium, The Philippines and South East Central Africa. He is married to Rosemary, with a son and daughter.

More Books from Brian Johnston

Brian has published over 70 books under the Search For Truth imprint, including:

Finding Christ in the Old Testament

"They said to one another, 'Were our hearts not burning within us when He was speaking to us on the road, while He was explaining the Scriptures to us?'" (Luke 24:27:32) Burning hearts! The inevitable result of having the Bible explained so it all begins to make sense and the person and work of Christ, its central character, comes into sharper focus. I used to think it would be wonderful to know what Old Testament incidents, symbols and themes the Lord unpacked for them. The way to do it seems obvious now! Wouldn't they be the same things that he and his Apostles spoke about - things that were later recorded and expounded in the New Testament? This book is the result of that thought process and picks up on these themes using as near as possible the order in which we encounter them in the Old Testament, including:

- Born of a Woman (Galatians 4:4)
- The Type of Him Who Was to Come (Romans 5:14)
- The Only Begotten Son (Hebrews 11:17-19)
- Christ Our Passover (1 Corinthians 5:7)

- The Bread That Came Out of Heaven (John 6:51)
- Sacrifice and Offering (Hebrews 10:5) & The Blood of Goats and Bulls (Hebrews 9:13)
- The Firstfruits
- The Ashes of a (Red) Heifer (Hebrews 9:13)
- The Bronze Serpent
- The King-Priest
- The Suffering Servant (1 Peter 2:24)
- Son of Man (Matthew 26:62)
- The Sign of Jonah (Matthew 12:39)

A Greater Sense of God: A Divine Invitation to Intimacy

On January 28, 1986, 7 Space Shuttle Challenger astronauts exited gravity and entered eternity. President Reagan gave quite a speech that day, paraphrasing the poetry of an Air Force volunteer: they "slipped the surly bonds of earth ... and touched the face of God." To touch the face of God suggests intimacy, as with someone we know well. In the Bible, we often find expressions such as "seeking God's face" to describe prayer, and occasionally "the softening of his face" which suggests soothing, possibly by touching. One of the most amazing revelations about God in the Bible is that he wants you and me to become intimate with him - and the goal of this book, starting with God's revelation to the prophet Ezekiel, is quite simply to help that become a reality.

The Journey of the Ark

In the days of Moses, God lived in the Tabernacle tent in the middle of his people – a portable structure that moved with them on their journey. It included the sacred chest known as the ark of the covenant, normally located in the holy innermost part of God's house which symbolized the Lord's presence. In this short book, Bible teacher Brian Johnston traces the ark's 500-year journey from Sinai to Zion and explains how the ark is a picture of the Lord Jesus who accompanies Christians on their spiritual journey, and gives lessons for our daily walk today.

Our God Reigns! The Awesome Sovereignty of God

"We are still masters of our fate. We still are captains of our souls," said Winston Churchill in World War 2, paraphrasing a fragment of a famous poem also admired by Nelson Mandela. Perhaps it's become a cultural meme, but is it in step with the Bible's theme? Can we control our own destiny, or is it all down to chance? Who, or what, is in charge of history?

To be credible, any worldview must answer four questions – about our origins, our morality, our (life's) meaning, and our destiny. When the author's daily Bible readings took him to Isaiah 37-47, he found the Biblical worldview does just that in an impressive declaration and demonstration of the sovereignty of God. That's what led to the writing of this book, which along the way seeks to answer some important questions that have puzzled people for centuries:

- What does the Bible categorically say about human origins?

- Does God change his mind?
- Why did God order the killing of peoples in the Old Testament?
- Has Israel been left out of God's purposes?
- Why bother praying?
- Was Jesus' crucifixion simply a terrible accident?
- Does God decide who is saved and who isn't?
- What are God's purposes in the end times?
- Does man have free wills?
- Do the sign gifts operate today in God's purposes?

About the Publisher

Hayes Press (www.hayespress.org) is a registered charity in the United Kingdom, whose primary mission is to disseminate the Word of God, mainly through literature. It is one of the largest distributors of gospel tracts and leaflets in the United Kingdom, with over 100 titles and many thousands dispatched annually. In addition to paperbacks and eBooks, Hayes Press also publishes Plus Eagles' Wings, a fun and educational Bible magazine for children, and Golden Bells, a popular daily Bible reading calendar in wall or desk formats.

If you would like to contact Hayes Press, there are a number of ways you can do so:

By mail: c/o The Barn, Flaxlands, Royal Wootton Bassett, Wiltshire, UK SN4 8DY

By phone: 01793 850598

By eMail: info@hayespress.org

via Facebook: www.facebook.com/hayespress.org